Table Of Contents

Introduction

Welcome to "Super Interesting Facts for Curious Kids"!

In this book, you'll find loads of fun facts about all kinds of cool things, from amazing animals and awesome inventions to exciting explorers and surprising customs. Our world is filled with wonderful mysteries waiting for you to discover, and this book will help you learn more about the things that make it special. So, get ready to explore, have fun, and always stay curious about the world around you!

The Human Body

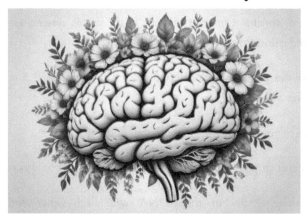

- The human nose can differentiate between over a trillion scents.

- Human bones are about five times stronger than steel of the same density.

- The liver can regenerate to its full size from as little as 25% of its original mass.

- Fingernails grow about three times faster than toenails.

- Babies have about 94 more bones than adults due to bone fusion over time.

- Your skeleton renews itself approximately every 10 years.

- The brain can store around 2.5 petabytes of data, enough to hold 3 million hours of TV shows.

- The digestive system is home to trillions of bacteria, known collectively as the gut microbiome.

- The tongue is covered in about 10,000 taste buds, which replace themselves every two weeks.

- The average adult body is made up of approximately 60% water.

- The small intestine is about 22 feet long, while the large intestine is around 5 feet.

- Human teeth are the only body part that cannot repair itself.

- Blood vessels in the human body could circle the globe twice if laid end to end.

- The surface area of a human lung is roughly the size of a tennis court.

- Your sense of smell is connected directly to the limbic system, associated with memory and emotions.

- The human heart beats about 100,000 times daily, pumping 1.5 million barrels of blood over a lifetime.

- About 25% of your bones are in your hands and feet.

- Your ears never stop growing throughout your life due to changes in cartilage.

- Humans share 99.9% of their DNA with each other and 96% with chimpanzees.

- The cornea is the only tissue in the body that doesn't have blood vessels.

- Human saliva contains natural painkillers called opiorphins, which are six times more powerful than morphine.

- The skin sheds about 30,000-40,000 dead cells every minute.

- The average human walks about 110,000 miles in their lifetime, or around five times around the Earth.

- During REM sleep, your body becomes effectively paralyzed to prevent acting out dreams.

- The human body contains around 37.2 trillion cells.

- The strongest muscle in the body, relative to its size, is the masseter or jaw muscle.

- Each human eye has about 107 million light-sensitive cells for detecting visual information.

- Taste is about 80% smell, which is why food tastes different when you have a cold.

- If your stomach lining didn't replace itself every 3-4 days, its acid would digest it.

- Human lips have more than a million nerve endings, making them extremely sensitive.

- Human beings are the only animals that cry emotional tears.

- The brain uses the same energy as a 10-watt light bulb while awake.

- Your body produces about a liter of mucus each day to protect your respiratory system.

- The sense of touch can detect pressure as light as 20 milligrams on the skin.

- The heart has its own electrical system, allowing it to continue beating outside of the body.

- Fingertips have a unique set of ridges known as fingerprints that no two people share.

- Blushing is caused by the sympathetic nervous system's response to embarrassment.

- The body's biological clock is called the suprachiasmatic nucleus, located in the hypothalamus.

- The longest muscle in the body is the sartorius, running down the length of the thigh.

- The shortest bone in the body is the stapes, found in the middle ear.

- More electrical impulses are generated in the brain each day than all the world's telephones combined.

- Human lungs contain about 300 million alveoli, or air sacs, for gas exchange.

- The human genome contains around 3 billion base pairs, making it an enormous storage system.

- Hair and nails continue to grow for a short period after death due to residual cellular activity.

- The gut is sometimes referred to as the "second brain" due to its network of neurons and neurotransmitters.

- The pancreas produces enzymes that break down carbohydrates, fats, and proteins in the small intestine.

- About 80% of brain mass is composed of water.

- The liver filters over a liter of blood per minute, removing toxins and regulating nutrients.

- On average, humans produce enough saliva each day to fill a wine bottle.

- Your brain generates more thoughts daily than the number of words in all the books ever published.

- A sneeze can travel at speeds of up to 100 mph.

- The brain is capable of processing information at a speed of about 120 meters per second.

- Human ears have tiny hairs called stereocilia that convert sound waves into nerve signals.

- Your tongue is home to various bacteria, some beneficial and others potentially harmful.

- Men's beards continue to grow faster than any other hair on their bodies.

- The optic nerve transmits visual information from the eyes to the brain at a speed of 37 mph.

- Your pupils can change size up to 45% when aroused.

- The average adult inhales and exhales approximately 22,000 times each day.

- There are about 2-5 million sweat glands in the human body.

- The placenta is the only organ that is grown temporarily.

- The eyes produce about 300 milliliters of tears annually, some emotional and some functional.

- The body's skin contains about 640,000 sensory receptors for touch.

- Your taste buds recognize five tastes: sweet, salty, bitter, sour, and umami.

- Hair on the head grows around 6 inches per year.

- The body's lymphatic system helps remove toxins and waste from the body.

- Human beings have a "dominant" nostril that is more active and switches every few hours.

- The bones of the middle ear are responsible for transmitting sound vibrations to the inner ear.

- The brain's hippocampus is crucial for memory formation and spatial navigation.

- Goosebumps occur due to tiny muscles at the base of each hair follicle.

- The pineal gland, located deep in the brain, helps regulate the sleep-wake cycle.

- Human bone marrow produces around 200 billion new blood cells each day.

- About 40% of the human brain is composed of gray matter, while the rest is white matter.

- The spleen filters the blood and helps fight certain bacteria.

- Earwax serves as a protective barrier to trap dirt, dust, and microorganisms.

- The average person has around 150,000 hairs on their scalp.

- Sweat itself is odorless; the smell comes from bacteria breaking down sweat compounds.

- The eyes contain specialized cells called rods and cones, which are responsible for night and color vision.

- The brain can recognize a face in just 13 milliseconds.

- The hypothalamus controls hunger, thirst, body temperature, and circadian rhythms.

- Your heartbeat syncs up with music if you're listening to it.

- The pituitary gland, often called the "master gland," controls various hormones in the body.

- The human stomach has about 35 million digestive glands.

- Human skin can detect a change in temperature as small as 0.01 degrees Celsius.

- The retina contains over 126 million photoreceptor cells.

- The ear contains tiny crystals called otoconia, which aid in balance.

- Your brain can't feel pain directly, as it lacks pain receptors.

- The appendix contains lymphatic tissue and may play a role in gut immunity.

- The Achilles tendon is the strongest and thickest tendon in the human body.

- The body naturally destroys and replaces about 1% of its red blood cells every day.

- The cerebral cortex is responsible for thought, perception, and memory storage.

- Hiccups occur when the diaphragm muscle contracts involuntarily.

- The retina processes visual information before sending it to the brain.

- Your eyes can distinguish up to 10 million colors.

- The spleen plays a key role in recycling iron from old red blood cells.

- The nasal cavity contains specialized nerve cells that are directly connected to the brain.

- Your vocal cords stretch up to 0.75 inches longer during a scream.

- The pancreas secretes insulin and glucagon, which regulate blood sugar levels.

- The sense of taste diminishes with age, particularly after the age of 60.

- Your jaw muscles can generate up to 200 pounds of force.

- The hypothalamus controls the release of hormones that regulate emotions and behavior.

The Animal Kingdom

- Wombat poop is cube-shaped to prevent it from rolling away, which is useful for marking their territory.

- Elephants use their trunks to detect underground vibrations.

- Dolphins sleep with one half of their brain while the other half remains alert.

- Crows can remember human faces and hold grudges against those who mistreat them.

- Tigers have striped skin, not just striped fur.

- Ants can carry objects 50 times their body weight.

- Koalas sleep up to 22 hours a day due to their low-energy diet.

- Penguins propose to their mates by offering them pebbles.

- Cats have a specialized collarbone that allows them to always land on their feet.

- Dogs' noses have unique patterns similar to human fingerprints.

- Giraffes have the same number of neck vertebrae as humans, just much longer.

- Pigeons can recognize their reflection in a mirror, indicating self-awareness.

- Octopuses can detach and regrow their arms if needed.

- Horses have a special locking mechanism in their legs that allows them to sleep standing up.

- Male seahorses carry and give birth to their offspring.

- Spiders can produce different types of silk for various purposes like webs and egg sacs.

- Owls have asymmetrical ears, which help them pinpoint the location of prey.

- Honeybees can communicate with each other using a complex "waggle dance."

- Rabbits eat their own droppings to re-digest nutrients.

- Bats are the only mammals capable of sustained flight.

- Wolves use facial expressions to communicate their status in the pack.

- Sharks have electroreceptive organs to detect the electrical fields of other organisms.

- Camels have three sets of eyelids and two rows of eyelashes to protect their eyes from sand.

- Lions' roars can be heard up to five miles away.

- Frogs can hibernate in mud for months if the water around them dries up.

- Beavers have transparent eyelids so they can see underwater while building dams.

- Parrots can mimic human speech due to their highly developed vocal organs.

- Male peacocks display elaborate tail feathers to attract females.

- Chimpanzees use sticks as tools to extract insects from nests.

- Squirrels are known to "fake bury" nuts to deceive potential thieves.

- Snakes have a highly flexible jaw that allows them to swallow prey whole.

- Eagles have eyesight up to four times sharper than that of humans.

- Zebras' stripes are unique to each individual, similar to fingerprints.

- Gorillas construct new nests every night using branches and leaves.

- Otters hold hands while sleeping to avoid drifting apart.

- Kangaroos can pause pregnancy and resume it when conditions improve.

- Hippos secrete a natural sunscreen that appears pinkish in color.

- Sea turtles navigate long distances using the Earth's magnetic field.

- Elephants mourn their dead and recognize elephant bones.

- Cheetahs can accelerate from 0 to 60 mph in just a few seconds.

- Dolphins have unique signature whistles that act like names.

- Polar bears have black skin underneath their white fur to absorb heat.

- Goats have rectangular pupils, giving them a wide field of vision.

- Kangaroos are incapable of walking backward due to their anatomy.

- Female octopuses sometimes sacrifice themselves to protect their eggs.

- Whales use complex songs to communicate and find mates.

- Snakes can sense the body heat of their prey through specialized pits.

- Hyenas have matriarchal societies where females are dominant over males.

- Elephants can recognize themselves in mirrors, showing self-awareness.

- Crocodiles can "cry" while eating due to air being forced out of their sinuses.

- Cats' purring may promote bone healing and reduce stress.

- Geese can form lifelong pair bonds and mourn the loss of their partners.

- Wolves use howling to maintain pack cohesion and locate each other.

- Crows use tools like sticks and leaves to extract insects from bark.

- Dogs can be trained to detect changes in blood sugar levels in diabetics.

- Bison are surprisingly agile and can jump over six feet vertically.

- Elephants communicate over long distances using infrasound.

- Sperm whales have the largest brain of any animal, weighing up to 17 pounds.

- Meerkats take turns acting as sentinels to watch for predators.

- Rabbits thump their hind legs to warn others of danger.

- Bearded dragons can change color to regulate body temperature and communicate.

- Wolves have scent glands between their toes to mark their territory.

- Dolphins' playful behavior is linked to strong social bonds and intelligence.

- Giraffes sleep only for short periods to avoid being vulnerable to predators.

- Bats use echolocation by emitting high-pitched sounds and analyzing echoes.

- Sharks can go for weeks or even months without eating.

- Capuchin monkeys use stones as hammers to crack nuts.

- Cats' whiskers can detect changes in their environment, helping them navigate.

- Male bowerbirds build elaborate structures to attract mates.

- Elephants' trunks can hold up to 2.5 gallons of water.

- Male emperor penguins incubate their eggs in freezing temperatures.

- Sloths have a specialized diet and can take days to digest food.

- Wolves and dogs can read human facial expressions and respond accordingly.

- Raccoons are highly dexterous and can open locks and jars.

- Octopuses can squeeze through small openings due to their soft bodies.

- Eagles can carry prey weighing up to half their body weight.

- Flamingos filter-feed by using their unique, upside-down beaks.

- Armadillos can curl up into a ball for protection against predators.

- Humpback whales create bubble nets to trap schools of fish.

- Ants communicate using chemical signals called pheromones.

- Elephants have highly developed temporal lobes, aiding memory.

- Baboons use facial expressions and vocalizations to establish dominance.

- Snakes shed their skin to accommodate growth and remove parasites.

- Koalas have fingerprints that closely resemble those of humans.

- Beavers' teeth grow continuously and are kept in check by gnawing.

- Orcas can "spyhop," or rise vertically out of the water to look around.

- Giraffes have specialized valves in their necks to manage blood flow to their brains.

- Ducks have waterproof feathers due to a gland that produces oil.

- Woodpeckers have reinforced skulls to protect their brains from impact.

- Orangutans can craft tools like leaves as umbrellas for rain protection.

- Elephants are capable of using basic arithmetic to solve problems.

- Seals can navigate by detecting Earth's magnetic field and follow ocean currents.

- Capybaras have a complex social structure with clear hierarchies.

- Lobsters communicate using urine released from their eye stalks.

- Swans mate for life and perform synchronized swimming displays.

- Chameleons change color to regulate body temperature and signal emotions.

- Dolphins engage in cooperative hunting, herding fish into tight balls.

- Camels can drink up to 40 gallons of water in one sitting.

- Narwhals use their long tusks to sense changes in water temperature and salinity.

- Orcas have regional dialects, meaning they "speak" differently based on their pod.

- Kangaroo rats can survive without drinking water by metabolizing the moisture in seeds.

Strange Traditions and Customs

- In Denmark, turning 25 without being married might lead to friends covering you in cinnamon, a quirky tradition known as "kanelvask."

- The Cooper's Hill Cheese-Rolling and Wake in England involves participants chasing a rolling wheel of cheese down a steep hill.

- During Spain's "La Tomatina," thousands gather to throw tons of ripe tomatoes at each other in a chaotic street fight.

- The monkey buffet festival in Thailand serves an extravagant feast of fruits and vegetables to local monkeys.

- In Papua New Guinea, some tribes perform a scarification ritual that mimics crocodile skin as a rite of passage into adulthood.

- In the Philippines, people jump as high as possible at midnight on New Year's Eve, hoping to grow taller in the coming year.

- The "El Colacho" festival in Spain has men dressed as devils jumping over rows of babies to cleanse them of sin.

- In Germany, newlyweds saw a log together at their wedding to demonstrate teamwork and cooperation.

- In Bolivia, the Tinku Festival features ritualistic fighting to honor Mother Earth with blood offerings.

- In Scotland, "first-footing" involves being the first to enter a house after midnight on New Year's Eve, often bearing gifts for good luck.

- In New Zealand, the Māori greet each other by pressing noses together in a practice called "hongi."

- South Korea's Pepero Day is celebrated by exchanging chocolate-covered sticks between couples and friends.

- During the Hindu festival of "Thaipusam," some devotees pierce their bodies to show devotion.

- In Greece, smashing plates during celebrations is a way to express joy and let loose.

- In Bolivia's Oruro Carnival, people wear elaborate masks and costumes to honor the Virgin of Socavón.

- In the Solomon Islands, whistling at night is considered bad luck because it may attract evil spirits.

- In Ireland, women place mistletoe under their pillows on New Year's Eve to dream about their future husbands.

- The Konyak Nagas in India celebrate their past headhunting culture by donning feathered headgear and dancing during the Aoling Festival.

- In Indonesia's "Ngaben" ceremony, Balinese Hindus conduct elaborate cremation rituals to release the soul into the afterlife.

- In Denmark, breaking dishes and leaving the shards at friends' doors on New Year's Eve signifies affection and luck.

- In Peru's "Festa de la Candelaria," musicians and dancers perform in honor of the Virgin Mary with elaborate costumes.

- In the Netherlands, people hang up a bag of school books when students pass their final exams.

- In Italy, La Befana is a friendly witch who delivers presents to children on Epiphany.

- The Henna Night in Turkey, held before a wedding, involves painting intricate henna patterns on the bride's hands and feet.

- In Japan, "Osechi Ryori" is a New Year's tradition of eating specially prepared, symbolically significant foods for prosperity.

- In Spain, people eat 12 grapes at midnight on New Year's Eve to ensure good luck for each month of the new year.

- The Krampuslauf in Austria involves people dressed as Krampus, the mythical creature, scaring children and causing mischief.

- In Switzerland, children compete to roll eggs down hills during the "Ostereier Tütsche" festival.

- In Brazil, people celebrate "Festa Junina" by dressing as farmers and square dancing to honor saints.

- During South Korea's "Chuseok" harvest festival, families visit ancestral graves to pay respects and share a traditional meal.

- In France, people eat crepes on "Le Jour des Crepes" and try flipping them with a coin in hand for good luck.

- In Spain, a traditional running of the bulls occurs during the San Fermin festival, attracting thousands of participants.

- The Timkat Festival in Ethiopia is a colorful religious celebration that commemorates the baptism of Jesus in the Jordan River.

- The Latvian "Jāņi" festival celebrates the summer solstice with bonfires, wreaths, and singing traditional songs.

- In Russia, people celebrate "Maslenitsa" with pancakes, sleigh rides, and games as they bid farewell to winter.

- The Scandinavian "kräftskiva" festival celebrates the crayfish harvest with traditional songs and schnapps.

- In Mexico, people eat tamales to mark "Dia de la Candelaria," which officially ends the Christmas season.

- During "Songkran," Thailand's New Year, people joyously splash water on each other in a symbolic cleansing.

- The Bun Festival in Hong Kong includes a race up a tower covered in sweet buns for prosperity.

- In Japan, "Setsubun" is celebrated by throwing beans out the door to chase away evil spirits.

- "Burning Man" is a countercultural festival in the Nevada desert where participants build and burn large-scale art installations.

- During the Brazilian Carnival, samba schools compete in elaborate parades to win the title of best samba performance.

Crazy Beliefs of the Past

- In the Middle Ages, some Europeans believed that a kiss from a donkey could cure a toothache.

- Ancient Romans thought that drinking gladiator blood could improve their strength and vitality.

- In the 19th century, doctors recommended smoking cigarettes to clear the lungs and prevent respiratory illness.

- People once believed that tomatoes, called "poison apples," could be fatal due to their acidic properties.

- Medieval Europeans thought that ringing church bells could disperse storms and keep lightning away.

- In ancient Egypt, it was believed that eating cabbage before a heavy drinking session would prevent a hangover.

- People thought that wearing an "abracadabra" amulet could ward off malaria and other diseases in the Middle Ages.

- Victorian-era doctors prescribed heroin as a cough suppressant and pain reliever.

- Some thought that placing a piece of iron under a bed would prevent witches from cursing the sleeper.

- In the 18th century, it was believed that bloodletting could cure most illnesses by balancing bodily humors.

- During the Renaissance, people believed that powdered human skulls could cure epilepsy and other ailments.

- Greeks and Romans believed that wearing amulets with stones or animal bones could protect against curses.

- In the early 20th century, it was thought that lobotomies could treat mental illnesses by "calming" the brain.

- Some believed that bathing in donkey milk would maintain youthful skin and cure various ailments.

- In ancient China, doctors thought that ingesting mercury could grant immortality but instead caused fatal poisoning.

- European alchemists tried to turn lead into gold, believing it was possible through mystical and chemical processes.

- People believed that if they swallowed a spider while sleeping, it would weave a web inside their stomach.

- In ancient Rome, wearing a lead disc around the neck was thought to protect against the evil eye.

- During the medieval period, women believed that carrying an onion under their armpit would help them conceive a child.

- Ancient Mesopotamians thought eclipses were a sign of the gods' wrath and would bring disaster.

- In the 19th century, parents believed that giving babies opium-laced "soothing syrups" would improve their sleep.

- People once believed that shaving one's head would help cure baldness.

- Ancient Greek doctors thought that women were more susceptible to hysteria because their wombs could "wander" around the body.

- People believed that wearing garlic around their necks would ward off vampires and other evil creatures.

- During the Victorian era, it was thought that tight corsets could cure curvature of the spine.

- Ancient Romans used crocodile dung as a beauty treatment and for medicinal purposes.

- In the Middle Ages, people believed that leeches could suck out evil spirits from the blood.

- It was believed that drinking snake oil would cure joint pain and various ailments.

- In ancient Greece, using sheep's wool as a bandage was thought to promote healing due to the wool's natural oils.

- Some believed that the position of moles on the body could predict one's fortune or character traits.

Pets are Amazing

- Cats have a specialized collarbone that allows them to twist their bodies mid-fall, ensuring they land on their feet.

- Dogs can learn over 1,000 words and gestures, recognizing meanings and commands.

- Cats purr at a frequency between 25 and 150 Hz, which has been shown to promote healing.

- Dogs' sense of smell is up to 100,000 times more sensitive than that of humans.

- Cats' whiskers are highly sensitive and can detect changes in their environment, such as the width of openings.

- Dogs' noses have unique ridge patterns, similar to human fingerprints.

- Cats have extra eyelids called haw or nictitating membranes, which help keep their eyes moist and protected.

- Dogs communicate with humans through facial expressions, eye contact, and tail wagging.

- Cats use various vocalizations, like meowing and chirping, primarily to communicate with humans.

- Dogs are capable of identifying their owner's emotions and will adjust their behavior accordingly.

- Cats can detect minute movements in the air with their whiskers, helping them hunt and navigate.

- Dogs have an innate ability to sense changes in human blood sugar levels and can alert diabetics.

- Cats' retractable claws stay sharp, making them efficient hunters and allowing silent movement.

- Dogs tilt their heads when listening to us because they are trying to locate the source of sounds.

- Cats have scent glands on their cheeks and will rub their faces on humans or objects to mark territory.

- Dogs' paws can detect temperature and surface textures, helping them navigate different terrains.

- Cats have a reflective layer in their eyes, the tapetum lucidum, which improves their night vision.

- Dogs can smell changes in human hormones, helping them detect stress, fear, and illness.

- Cats are capable of running up to 30 mph for short distances.

- Dogs experience a form of jealousy and can respond negatively when their owners give attention to other pets or people.

- Cats' purring can act as a self-soothing mechanism, often used when they're stressed or unwell.

- Dogs have an instinct to circle before lying down, a behavior inherited from their wild ancestors.

- Cats have 32 muscles in each ear, allowing them to rotate their ears independently to detect sounds.

- Dogs have specialized cone cells that make them dichromatic, seeing a color spectrum of blue and yellow.

- Cats groom themselves frequently to spread natural oils and regulate their body temperature.

- Dogs' licking releases endorphins, which reduces stress and calms them down.

- Cats can jump up to six times their body length from a standing position.

- Dogs have sweat glands only on their paw pads, which is why they pant to cool down.

- Cats recognize their owner's voice but may ignore it out of selective attention.

- Dogs' play behavior, like fetching, mimics hunting strategies and is rooted in instinct.

- Cats can sleep up to 16 hours a day to conserve energy for hunting.

- Dogs can learn to identify specific people or animals by scent alone, even from long distances.

- Cats knead with their paws as a comforting behavior, reminiscent of nursing.

- Dogs' tails wag to the right when they are happy and to the left when they are anxious.

- Cats can detect seismic activity, sometimes hours before earthquakes occur.

- Dogs can recognize their owner's face among other humans, even in photos.

- Cats' flexible spine allows them to twist and stretch to clean hard-to-reach areas.

- Dogs use their tails to communicate their emotions, like excitement, fear, or aggression.

- Cats will often bring their owners "gifts" of prey as a token of affection and to share resources.

- Dogs have a vomeronasal organ, or Jacobson's organ, which detects pheromones.

- Cats prefer a clean litter box because they have an acute sense of smell.

- Dogs can hear higher-pitched sounds than humans, which is why they respond to dog whistles.

- Cats have a unique grooming ritual that often involves licking themselves in a specific sequence.

- Dogs' powerful sense of smell allows them to detect certain types of cancer in humans.

- Cats can suffer from separation anxiety when their owners are away for extended periods.

- Dogs can distinguish between identical twins by scent, even when they eat the same diet.

- Cats are obligate carnivores and require a diet rich in animal proteins.

- Dogs will bark in different ways to convey specific messages, like playfulness or alarm.

- Cats' rough tongues are covered with papillae, which helps them remove loose fur and debris.

- Dogs have an innate understanding of human pointing gestures, even without training.

- Cats can memorize the location of objects they've seen moved out of their view.

- Dogs can develop phobias similar to humans, including fear of loud noises like thunderstorms.

- Cats are highly territorial and will defend their home turf against intruders.

- Dogs are social animals and often thrive in households with consistent human companionship.

- Cats have an incredible balance due to their inner ear structure, allowing them to walk along narrow edges.

- Dogs can recognize different languages and commands, understanding the tone of voice used.

- Cats are often crepuscular, meaning they are most active at dawn and dusk.

- Dogs can detect epileptic seizures before they occur due to subtle changes in their owner's behavior.

- Cats will often "chatter" at birds, possibly out of frustration from not being able to hunt them.

- Dogs can be trained to respond to gestures and hand signals, even in noisy environments.

- Cats' eyes have slit-shaped pupils, which provide better depth perception in low light.

- Dogs can understand the concept of time and will anticipate their owner's return at certain hours.

- Cats' scratching behavior helps them stretch, sharpen their claws, and mark territory.

- Dogs' skin is much thinner than human skin, making them more susceptible to cuts and bruises.

- Cats' tail flicking can indicate different emotions, like annoyance, excitement, or curiosity.

- Dogs' loyalty is rooted in their pack mentality, viewing their humans as members of the pack.

- Cats can rotate their ears 180 degrees to hear sounds from multiple directions.

- Dogs often mimic their owners' moods, becoming more energetic or subdued.

- Cats' low, rumbling purr can also be used to comfort their owners.

- Dogs can detect low blood pressure and alert their owners to sit down before fainting.

- Cats prefer their food at room temperature and may avoid eating chilled food.

- Dogs' hearing is sensitive to high frequencies, allowing them to detect sounds we can't.

- Cats will head-butt or "bunt" their owners to leave their scent and mark them as part of their territory.

- Dogs' saliva contains enzymes that help heal wounds and fight bacteria.

- Cats have five toes on their front paws but only four on their hind paws.

- Dogs' body language, like tail position and ear posture, conveys different emotional states.

- Cats' eyes can change color slightly with age or due to health conditions.

- Dogs often "smile" by pulling back their lips when relaxed and happy.

- Cats have a natural aversion to water because their fur takes time to dry, making them feel cold and vulnerable.

- Dogs will often wag their tails more vigorously when seeing their owners compared to strangers.

- Cats' long tails help them balance, particularly when climbing or jumping.

- Dogs' sense of smell is sensitive enough to detect diseases like Parkinson's and COVID-19.

- Cats' purring frequency can increase when they are hungry or seeking attention.

- Dogs will often lay their head on their owner's lap to seek comfort or reassurance.

- Cats can see a wider field of vision than humans, up to 200 degrees.

- Dogs' brains light up in MRI scans when they hear their owner's voice.

- Cats can form lifelong bonds with their owners, showing preference over strangers.

- Dogs' protective instincts make them excellent guard animals when trained correctly.

- Cats can be trained to walk on a leash, similar to dogs, but require patience.

- Dogs will sometimes lick their owner's face to communicate affection or request attention.

- Cats can detect slight shifts in the weather, often seeking shelter before a storm.

- Dogs' rapid panting can help them cool down by evaporating moisture from their tongue.

- Cats' meows can vary in pitch and duration, depending on their message.

- Dogs have been found to reduce their owner's stress levels and boost mood.

- Cats often bring their owners gifts as a way to share their hunting success.

- Dogs' playful nature can strengthen the bond between them and their owners.

- Cats are known to follow their owners from room to room, preferring their company.

- Dogs often curl up to conserve body heat and protect their vital organs.

- Cats' ears can detect ultrasonic frequencies, which are inaudible to humans.

- Dogs have a spatial awareness that helps them navigate environments without bumping into things.

Space and Planets

- A day on Venus is longer than a year on Venus due to its extremely slow rotation.

- The footprints left by astronauts on the Moon will remain for millions of years since there is no atmosphere or wind.

- One tablespoon of a neutron star would weigh about 1 billion tons on Earth.

- There are more stars in the universe than grains of sand on all of Earth's beaches.

- The Great Red Spot on Jupiter is a giant storm that has been raging for at least 400 years.

- Saturn's rings are mostly made of water ice, with some dust and rock mixed in.

- There is a planet named HD 189733b that rains glass sideways due to its extreme winds.

- One year on Neptune is equivalent to 165 Earth years because of its long orbit.

- Mars has the largest volcano in the solar system, Olympus Mons, which is about three times the height of Mount Everest.

- There are more than 200 moons orbiting planets in our solar system.

- The Sun contains 99.8% of the mass in our entire solar system.

- Black holes can stretch time itself due to their immense gravitational pull.

- Mercury experiences temperature fluctuations from -173°C to 427°C due to its lack of atmosphere.

- Pluto, now classified as a dwarf planet, has five known moons.

- The Milky Way galaxy is estimated to have over 100 billion stars.

- A day on Mercury lasts 59 Earth days, while a year lasts just 88 days.

- The solar wind, a stream of charged particles from the Sun, creates auroras when interacting with Earth's magnetic field.

- The surface of Mars appears reddish due to iron oxide, or rust, on its surface.

- The farthest human-made object from Earth is the Voyager 1 spacecraft, which has traveled beyond the solar system.

- The International Space Station orbits Earth every 90 minutes, giving astronauts 16 sunrises and sunsets daily.

- Saturn is so light that it would float in water if a large enough body of water were available.

- The Hubble Space Telescope has helped identify galaxies over 13 billion years old.

- Enceladus, a moon of Saturn, has geysers that spray water vapor and ice particles into space.

- The Kuiper Belt, a region beyond Neptune, contains many icy objects, including dwarf planets like Pluto.

- The Earth's magnetic field protects us from harmful solar radiation.

- Neptune has the fastest winds in the solar system, reaching speeds over 1,200 mph.

- The observable universe is estimated to be 93 billion light-years in diameter.

- Comets are icy bodies that release gas and dust when they approach the Sun, forming a bright tail.

- The Moon is slowly moving away from Earth at a rate of about 1.5 inches per year.

- Venus has a thick atmosphere composed mainly of carbon dioxide, causing a runaway greenhouse effect.

- The largest canyon in the solar system is Valles Marineris on Mars, which is over 2,500 miles long.

- The Sun will eventually become a red giant, expanding to engulf the inner planets, including Earth.

- Mars has seasons similar to Earth because its axis is tilted relative to its orbit.

- Jupiter's moon Europa is believed to have a vast ocean beneath its icy crust.

- The nearest star system to Earth is Alpha Centauri, about 4.37 light-years away.

- Saturn's moon Titan has lakes and rivers of liquid methane and ethane.

- The temperature at the core of the Sun can reach 15 million degrees Celsius.

- There is a giant hexagonal storm on Saturn's north pole that is visible from space.

- Neptune appears blue due to the presence of methane gas in its atmosphere.

- The gravity on the Moon is only about one-sixth that of Earth's, allowing astronauts to jump higher.

- Uranus is the only planet that orbits the Sun on its side, with a tilt of 98 degrees.

- The Milky Way is part of a local group of galaxies that includes Andromeda, which will collide with the Milky Way in 4 billion years.

- The ISS is a collaborative effort involving 15 nations and has been continuously inhabited since 2000.

- The Kuiper Belt is home to Eris, a dwarf planet once considered to be larger than Pluto.

- Asteroids are rocky remnants left over from the formation of the solar system.

- The solar system formed around 4.6 billion years ago from a collapsing gas and dust cloud.

- The James Webb Space Telescope, scheduled to launch in 2021, will observe the universe in infrared wavelengths.

- The largest moon in the solar system is Ganymede, which is even bigger than Mercury.

- Quasars are some of the brightest and most distant objects in the universe.

- The Martian atmosphere is so thin that liquid water cannot exist on its surface for long periods.

- Jupiter's magnetic field is 20,000 times stronger than Earth's, creating intense radiation belts.

- Space is not completely empty but contains about one atom per cubic centimeter in interstellar space.

- The Crab Nebula is the remnant of a supernova explosion observed by Chinese astronomers in 1054 AD.

- The Oort Cloud is a distant region of icy bodies surrounding our solar system, thought to be a source of comets.

- Earth experiences about 100 tons of space debris, mostly dust and meteoroids, falling to the surface daily.

- A single neutron star can emit more energy in a second than the Sun does in a million years.

- Jupiter's moon Io is the most volcanically active body in the solar system.

- The surface of the dwarf planet Ceres is thought to contain large amounts of water ice.

- The solar corona, the outermost layer of the Sun's atmosphere, is hotter than the Sun's surface.

- Mercury has no moons, unlike most of the other planets.

- The Moon has "moonquakes" caused by tidal forces from Earth's gravitational pull.

- The closest galaxy to the Milky Way is the Andromeda Galaxy, which is on a collision course with ours.

- The temperature on Venus is hot enough to melt lead, with average surface temperatures reaching 464°C.

- The first artificial satellite, Sputnik 1, was launched by the Soviet Union in 1957.

- The surface of Venus is hidden beneath thick clouds of sulfuric acid, making it difficult to observe directly.

- The Sun will end its life as a white dwarf, a small, dense remnant of its former self.

- The closest known black hole to Earth is about 1,000 light-years away in the HR 6819 system.

- Mars has two small moons, Phobos and Deimos, which are thought to be captured asteroids.

- Our Solar System resides in the Orion Arm of the Milky Way galaxy.

- The temperature on Uranus can drop as low as -224°C, making it the coldest planet in the solar system.

- Earth is the only known planet where plate tectonics actively shape the surface.

- The farthest planet visible to the naked eye is Uranus, under ideal viewing conditions.

- The Perseid meteor shower, one of the most well-known meteor showers, peaks each August as Earth passes through comet debris.

- The largest volcano on Earth, Mauna Kea, would be taller than Mount Everest if measured from its base on the ocean floor.

- Venus rotates in the opposite direction to most other planets, a phenomenon known as retrograde rotation.

- The Milky Way is on a collision course with the Andromeda Galaxy, which will form a new galaxy in about 4 billion years.

- The Sun's energy output is so powerful that it could power Earth's current energy needs for a million years in just one second.

- There is a supermassive black hole at the center of the Milky Way, known as Sagittarius A*.

- The outer planets are known as gas giants because they are composed mainly of hydrogen and helium.

- Earth's magnetic field, generated by its molten iron core, protects us from solar radiation.

- Saturn's moon Enceladus has geysers that eject water into space, creating a plume visible from orbit.

- The solar wind travels at speeds of up to 900 km/s, creating the heliosphere that surrounds the solar system.

- The Hubble Space Telescope has taken images of over 1 million celestial objects.

- The distance from the Sun to Earth is defined as an astronomical unit (AU) and is about 93 million miles.

- The largest asteroid in the asteroid belt, Ceres, is classified as a dwarf planet.

- Mercury is shrinking slowly over time as it cools and contracts.

- The "dark side of the Moon" is a misnomer, as both sides receive sunlight at different times.

- The star Betelgeuse, which is visible from Earth, is a red supergiant nearing the end of its life.

- A day on Uranus lasts about 17 hours due to its rapid rotation.

- The Cassini spacecraft orbited Saturn for 13 years before being deliberately crashed into the planet in 2017.

- The solar eclipse of 1919 was used to prove Einstein's theory of general relativity by showing how gravity bends light.

- The Moon has no atmosphere, so the sky always appears black, even during the lunar day.

- Some stars, known as pulsars, emit regular radio signals that can be detected from Earth.

- The surface of Pluto is covered in nitrogen ice and methane, with towering mountains made of water ice.

- The "Goldilocks zone" is the habitable region around a star where liquid water can exist on a planet's surface.

- Earth's rotation is gradually slowing due to tidal interactions with the Moon.

- The largest known galaxy, IC 1101, is estimated to be over 6 million light-years in diameter.

- The first interstellar object detected passing through our solar system was 'Oumuamua, discovered in 2017.

- The Sun is classified as a G-type main-sequence star, also known as a yellow dwarf.

- The first animals to orbit Earth were a pair of dogs named Belka and Strelka, launched by the Soviet Union in 1960.

Strange World Records

- The longest anyone has gone without sleep is 11 days, a record set in 1964.

- The world record for the longest hiccuping session is 68 years.

- The human body can survive without food for up to 70 days, given adequate water intake.

- The world record for the longest underwater breath-hold is over 24 minutes.

- The fastest mile run while wearing a straightjacket is just under 7 minutes.

- The longest time anyone has ever held a plank is over 9 hours.

- The most push-ups completed in an hour is 3,182.

- The longest someone has held their breath in ice-cold water is just under 12 minutes.

- The highest number of pull-ups completed in 24 hours is over 7,600.

- The world record for the longest marathon dance session is 126 hours.

- The longest distance someone has run on a treadmill in 24 hours is over 264 miles.

- The world record for solving a Rubik's cube blindfolded is under 17 seconds.

- The longest continuous juggling time without dropping is over 12 hours.

- The fastest anyone has typed the alphabet on a keyboard is under 2 seconds.

- The farthest someone has walked on their hands in 8 hours is over 17 miles.

- The longest continuous guitar playing session lasted over 114 hours.

- The most burpees completed in 12 hours is 5,755.

- The world record for continuous high-fiving is 30 hours.

- The most skips completed with a jump rope in 24 hours is 228,000.

- The world record for the longest applause is 2 hours and 5 minutes.

- The highest number of head spins done in a minute is 121.

- The longest time anyone has continuously dribbled a basketball is 26 hours.

- The most T-shirts worn at once is 260.

- The longest time anyone has continuously watched TV is over 94 hours.

- The longest distance run barefoot on snow is over 40 miles.

- The longest session of singing continuously lasted 101 hours.

- The most coconuts smashed with the head in one minute is 35.

- The most spoons balanced on the face simultaneously is 31.

- The longest continuous surfing session lasted over 30 hours.

- The highest number of candles blown out with one breath is 151.

- The longest time spent inside a bubble was 12 hours.

- The world record for running backwards a marathon is just over 3 hours and 53 minutes.

- The longest anyone has continuously stared at the sun without blinking is just over an hour.

- The most layers of socks worn at once is 252.

- The longest time anyone has continuously played chess is 50 hours.

- The fastest someone has solved a 4x4x4 Rubik's cube is under 16 seconds.

- The most matches lit with one hand in a minute is 115.

- The world record for juggling chainsaws is 94 catches.

- The most times a single person has completed a triathlon is 346.

- The most times someone has thrown a playing card in a minute is 114.

- The longest time spent in a barrel going down a waterfall is 4 minutes and 27 seconds.

- The most people someone has hugged in an hour is 1,749.

- The highest number of one-arm push-ups completed in an hour is 3,416.

- The longest anyone has continuously walked on stilts is 92 miles.

- The most somersaults on a trampoline in a minute is 69.

- The most drum beats played in 60 seconds is 2,370.

- The longest time anyone has continuously performed magic tricks is 72 hours.

- The highest number of dice balanced on a chopstick in one minute is 123.

- The most double Dutch jumps completed in 30 seconds is 201.

- The fastest anyone has completed a half-marathon while dribbling a soccer ball is 1 hour and 24 minutes.

- The most tennis balls juggled simultaneously is 11.

- The longest someone has hung upside down is 3 hours and 25 minutes.

- The fastest time anyone has peeled and eaten a lemon is 8.25 seconds.

- The highest number of one-finger push-ups completed in a minute is 19.

- The longest time anyone has continuously read aloud is 124 hours.

- The most watermelons chopped on a stomach in one minute is 25.

- The longest journey taken on a pogo stick is over 2,100 miles.

- The most bench presses completed in an hour is 1,186.

- The fastest anyone has eaten a bowl of spaghetti is 26.69 seconds.

- The highest number of straws stuffed into someone's mouth is 650.

- The longest time anyone has continuously slept is 11 days.

- The fastest anyone has written the entire English alphabet is 3.37 seconds.

- The longest someone has walked continuously without stopping is 310 miles.

- The most glasses balanced on the chin is 93.

- The highest number of simultaneous cartwheels completed is 2,204.

- The most chin-ups completed in a minute is 57.

- The longest someone has continuously clapped is 58 hours.

- The highest number of paper planes caught blindfolded in 3 minutes is 11.

- The most slices of bread buttered in one minute is 14.

- The longest swim in open water was 139.8 miles.

- The longest anyone has continuously cycled without sleep is 486 hours.

- The most balloons burst using only teeth in one minute is 30.

- The fastest anyone has climbed 100 meters of rope is 9.44 seconds.

- The longest anyone has stood on one foot is over 76 hours.

- The most pumpkins carved in an hour is 109.

- The longest time anyone has continuously played pool is 100 hours.

- The most basketball free throws made blindfolded in a minute is 10.

- The longest someone has continuously balanced on a Swiss ball is 7 hours and 7 minutes.

- The most eggs crushed with the head in one minute is 80.

- The longest marathon playing air guitar is 26 hours.

- The fastest someone has completed a mile hopping on one leg is just over 12 minutes.

- The longest anyone has continuously played darts is 48 hours.

- The highest number of yoga poses completed in a minute is 23.

- The longest someone has continuously spun a basketball on their nose is 7.7 seconds.

- The longest anyone has held a front lever position is 2 minutes and 10 seconds.

- The fastest anyone has solved a 3x3x3 Rubik's cube with one hand is under 10 seconds.

- The most flying kicks performed in a minute is 76.

- The fastest anyone has tied a shoelace is 15.51 seconds.

- The longest time someone has continuously practiced tai chi is 36 hours.

- The fastest someone has opened and closed an umbrella 30 times is 14.74 seconds.

- The most pairs of socks put on in 30 seconds is 28.

- The longest distance crawled on hands and knees is over 34 miles.

- The longest distance run barefoot is over 238 miles.

- The most marshmallows caught in the mouth in one minute is 58.

- The fastest someone has assembled a Mr. Potato Head blindfolded is 16.23 seconds.

- The longest someone has continuously danced is 123 hours.

- The longest anyone has held a bridge position is 4 hours and 1 minute.

- The fastest anyone has eaten a whole cucumber is 8.3 seconds.

- The most grapes eaten in three minutes is 205.

- The longest time anyone has continuously hopped on a pogo stick is 20 hours and 13 minutes.

- The most layers of toilet paper unrolled in 30 seconds is 7.

- The fastest time anyone has completed 100 push-ups is 46.61 seconds.

- The fastest anyone has sorted a deck of cards is 14.75 seconds.

- The longest someone has continuously balanced a chainsaw on their chin is 20 minutes and 40 seconds.

- The longest anyone has held a human flag position is 1 minute and 15 seconds.

- The longest distance run while balancing a baseball bat on the chin is 7.2 miles.

- The fastest anyone has eaten three cream crackers is 34.78 seconds.

- The fastest someone has stacked 10 cookies is 30.9 seconds.

- The longest time anyone has continuously typed is 134 hours.

- The longest someone has balanced a guitar on their chin is 3 hours and 9 minutes.

- The longest anyone has spun a plate on a stick is 10 hours.

- The most push-ups completed in one minute is 140.

- The longest time anyone has continuously flown a kite is 180 hours.

- The fastest time anyone has written 100 words in a single minute is 160.

- The most watermelons chopped with a sword in one minute is 27.

- The longest time someone has continuously played poker is 115 hours.

- The fastest anyone has opened 24 bottles of beer is 1 minute and 37 seconds.

Mind-Blowing Inventions

- Alexander Graham Bell, known for inventing the telephone, considered it a distraction and refused to have one in his office.

- Thomas Edison's most profitable invention was the electric pen, which laid the foundation for modern tattooing.

- The first windshield wiper was invented by Mary Anderson after noticing that drivers had to manually clear snow and rain.

- Leonardo da Vinci conceptualized a robotic knight in the 15th century, an early precursor to modern robotics.

- Nikola Tesla envisioned a "World Wireless System" for transmitting information across the globe, which anticipated Wi-Fi and the internet.

- The first electric chair was designed by a dentist, Dr. Alfred Southwick, who was inspired by accidental electrocutions.

- The ballpoint pen was invented by László Bíró to prevent ink smudging while writing quickly.

- Japanese inventor Yoshiro Nakamatsu claims to have invented a waterproof notepad for writing ideas while in the bathtub.

- Percy Spencer discovered how to use microwaves for cooking by accident while testing radar equipment, leading to the microwave oven.

- Margaret Knight, known as the "woman Edison," created a machine that produced flat-bottomed paper bags.

- The "cat piano" was a bizarre instrument with cats in cages, each meowing at different pitches when poked, allegedly intended to treat melancholia.

- George de Mestral invented Velcro after noticing how burdock burrs stuck to his dog's fur.

- Tim Berners-Lee invented the World Wide Web in 1989 as a means of sharing information among scientists.

- James Dyson made over 5,000 prototypes before finalizing the first bagless vacuum cleaner.

- A precursor to the modern bra was patented in 1914 by Mary Phelps Jacob after she disliked the look of corsets under evening gowns.

- The "baby cage," an unusual invention in 1930s England, allowed city-dwelling infants to nap outdoors by hanging them out the window.

- The first webcam, created in 1991, monitored a coffee pot in a university lab to check if it was full.

- Garrett Morgan invented the traffic signal after witnessing an accident at an intersection.

- The smiley face was created by Harvey Ball in 1963 for an insurance company's morale campaign.

- The first 3D printer, developed by Chuck Hull in the 1980s, revolutionized manufacturing by creating three-dimensional objects layer by layer.

- The "personal submarine," a portable submersible vehicle, was designed to explore coral reefs for leisure divers.

- The foldable umbrella was first patented by Samuel Fox in 1852 after noticing the need for a lighter, portable version.

- A famous medieval invention, "Greek fire," was a mysterious incendiary weapon used by the Byzantine Empire, known for burning even on water.

- The color mauve was discovered by accident by William Perkin when he was trying to synthesize quinine for malaria treatment.

- James Watt's separate condenser greatly improved steam engines, helping drive the Industrial Revolution.

- The "bathroom banjo," an eccentric invention, was designed to provide entertainment while using the toilet.

- Ruth Wakefield invented chocolate chip cookies when she added broken chocolate bars to her cookie dough.

- Charles Goodyear accidentally invented vulcanized rubber after spilling sulfur on hot rubber and noticing its improved properties.

- An unusual invention called "piano stairs" encourages physical activity by emitting piano sounds as people step on them.

- The first programmable computer, the "Analytical Engine," was conceptualized by Charles Babbage in the 1830s.

- The can opener was invented nearly 50 years after the tin can itself.

- The frisbee was inspired by empty pie tins thrown for fun at Yale University.

- Josephine Cochrane invented the first dishwasher in 1886 because she was frustrated by servants damaging her china.

- The "pet rock," a novelty fad in the 1970s, was simply a smooth stone sold with care instructions.

- Edward Jenner developed the smallpox vaccine in the late 18th century after noticing that milkmaids who had cowpox were immune to smallpox.

- Louis Braille developed the Braille writing system for the blind in 1824, using raised dots to represent letters.

- The first mechanical computer, known as the "Difference Engine," was never fully constructed due to funding issues.

- The "Duck Foot" pistol, invented in the 18th century, had multiple barrels to shoot in different directions at once.

- The earliest known vending machine dispensed holy water in temples of ancient Egypt in exchange for a coin.

- The "selfie stick" was first envisioned in a 1995 book, "101 Un-Useless Japanese Inventions," by Kenji Kawakami.

- John Walker accidentally invented matches after a stick used to stir chemicals ignited from friction.

- Earle Dickson invented Band-Aids for his wife, who often cut herself while cooking.

- The "nose stylus" was designed so people could operate smartphones with their noses in cold weather while wearing gloves.

- George Washington Carver discovered hundreds of uses for peanuts, including peanut butter, cosmetics, and rubber.

- The thermos flask, designed to keep liquids hot or cold, was invented by Scottish scientist James Dewar in the 1890s.

- Willis Carrier invented air conditioning after being tasked with reducing humidity in a printing plant.

- The "mousetrap boat," developed in the early 20th century, was meant to capture rodents while floating down a river.

- Sir Isaac Newton invented the cat door to allow his feline companions free movement in and out of his study.

- Galileo Galilei improved the telescope to 20x magnification, enabling significant astronomical discoveries.

- The "banana peeler," a humorous gadget, was designed to peel bananas despite their already user-friendly packaging.

The Foods We Eat

- Honey never spoils and has been found in ancient Egyptian tombs, still perfectly edible.

- Bananas are technically berries, while strawberries are not.

- The world's most expensive coffee, kopi luwak, is made from beans excreted by civet cats.

- Chocolate was used as currency by the ancient Aztecs.

- Carrots were originally purple before the Dutch cultivated the orange variety.

- The average American consumes about 23 pounds of ice cream per year.

- Cheese is the most stolen food item globally.

- Gelatin, a common ingredient in jelly, is derived from animal collagen.

- Apples float in water because they are made of 25% air.

- Nutmeg can be toxic if consumed in large quantities.

- Peanuts are not true nuts but legumes related to beans.

- Worcestershire sauce is made from anchovies that have been fermented for 18 months.

- Cashews grow on the outside of a fruit called a cashew apple.

- Potatoes were once considered poisonous by Europeans due to their relation to nightshade plants.

- Vanilla flavoring is derived from orchids and is one of the most labor-intensive crops to grow.

- Tomato ketchup was sold as a medicine in the 1830s.

- Black pepper was once so valuable that it was used as currency.

- The most expensive spice in the world is saffron, which comes from the stigma of the crocus flower.

- White chocolate is not truly chocolate since it contains no cocoa solids.

- Fortune cookies originated in California, not China.

- Figs often contain dead wasps, which pollinate the fruit.

- Apples are part of the rose family, along with pears and plums.

- The popsicle was invented by an 11-year-old in 1905 who accidentally left a drink outside overnight.

- The watermelon is a berry called a "pepo," while raspberries are classified as aggregate fruits.

- Almonds are seeds of the drupe fruit, not nuts.

- Ketchup was once believed to have medicinal properties and was marketed as a cure for indigestion.

- Arachibutyrophobia is the fear of peanut butter sticking to the roof of one's mouth.

- One teaspoon of soil can contain more bacteria than there are people on Earth.

- Butter was once considered a luxury item in ancient Rome and was used as medicine.

- Pufferfish or "fugu" is a delicacy in Japan that can be lethal if prepared incorrectly.

- Coconuts kill more people annually than sharks do.

- Casu marzu, a traditional Sardinian cheese, is made with live insect larvae.

- Peppers are rated by heat using the Scoville scale, named after pharmacist Wilbur Scoville.

- Bread was used as an eraser before rubber was developed.

- Coconut water was used as an emergency blood plasma substitute during World War II.

- The durian fruit, known as the "king of fruits," is banned in many public places due to its strong odor.

- Edible gold is a luxury ingredient used to garnish gourmet dishes.

- An average ear of corn has about 800 kernels, arranged in 16 rows.

- Spam is especially popular in Hawaii, which consumes more than any other state in the U.S.

- Truffles are fungi that grow underground and are harvested with the help of trained pigs or dogs.

- The "white whale" of coffee beans, the rare Panama Geisha, sells for over $800 per pound.

- Applesauce was the first food eaten by astronauts in space.

- Kiwifruit originated in China and was originally known as the Chinese gooseberry.

- Cucumbers consist of 96% water, making them one of the most hydrating vegetables.

- Vanilla ice cream was once considered exotic and rare before it became mainstream.

- Pineapples contain an enzyme called bromelain that breaks down proteins, tenderizing meat.

- Most commercial wasabi is just horseradish with food coloring.

- Bubblegum was initially created by an accountant experimenting with chewing gum recipes.

- Caviar was once a cheap bar snack in the U.S. before becoming a delicacy.

- The ancient Greeks and Romans used honey as an offering to their gods.

- Graham crackers were originally invented as a health food to curb sexual urges.

- The largest pumpkin pie ever made weighed over 3,699 pounds.

- One teaspoon of honey requires the work of about 12 honey bees.

- Black sapote, also known as the "chocolate pudding fruit," tastes like sweet cocoa.

- Olive oil was used in ancient Greece as a skincare product and currency.

- The earliest known recipe dates back to ancient Mesopotamia, describing how to brew beer.

- Bird's nest soup, a delicacy in Asia, is made from the hardened saliva of swiftlet birds.

- The molecular structure of caffeine is very similar to that of adenosine, which calms brain activity.

- Mushrooms are more closely related to humans than to plants genetically.

- Almond milk was a popular ingredient in medieval European recipes as a dairy substitute.

- Cheese production dates back over 7,200 years to ancient Poland.

- The Japanese "fugu" chef must complete rigorous training before being licensed to prepare pufferfish.

- A single can of soda can contain up to 10 teaspoons of sugar.

- French fries originated in Belgium, not France.

- Lobsters were once so abundant in North America that they were fed to prisoners and servants.

- Avocados are the only fruit that contains healthy fats and no sugar.

- Maple syrup was first used by Native Americans as a sweetener and medicinal ingredient.

- The green color of wasabi leaves comes from chlorophyll, but the root itself is white.

- Pine nuts come from the seeds of pine trees and are a staple in pesto sauce.

- The peanut plant flowers above ground, but its nuts grow underground.

- The average American consumes 22 pounds of tomatoes per year, mostly as ketchup or sauce.

- The Oreo cookie is the most popular cookie in the world.

- In 1900s America, sugar was advertised as a weight-loss ingredient.

- Ancient Egyptians considered onions to be sacred and often used them in burial rituals.

- The milkshake was originally an alcoholic beverage made with whiskey and eggs.

- Some studies suggest that eating dark chocolate may improve brain function.

- The hamburger originated in Hamburg, Germany, but became popular in the U.S.

- Potatoes contain more potassium than bananas.

- The original Caesar salad was created in Tijuana, Mexico, not Italy.

- Miso soup contains probiotics, which can promote gut health.

- Sweet potatoes and yams are not botanically related, despite their similar appearance.

- Humans have been fermenting foods and beverages for at least 9,000 years.

- Crickets are an emerging source of protein and are often ground into flour.

- Table salt can be derived from seawater or mined from underground deposits.

- In Japan, Kit Kat bars come in over 300 flavors, including wasabi, green tea, and soy sauce.

- Red wine contains antioxidants that may have heart health benefits when consumed in moderation.

- Buffalo wings were invented at a bar in Buffalo, New York, in the 1960s.

- The world's largest pizza measured over 13,580 square feet.

- Nutella was invented during World War II due to a shortage of cocoa.

- Raw oysters can change their gender multiple times throughout their lives.

- The pistachio nut is technically a seed and is related to cashews.

- Rice paper, used in Asian spring rolls, is made from the pith of rice plants.

- Bananas emit a gas called ethylene, which speeds up the ripening process of nearby fruits.

- Ancient Peruvians preserved potatoes by freeze-drying them, creating chuño.

- Coffee beans are actually the seeds of the coffee cherry.

- Jellybeans were sent to soldiers during the Civil War as a source of sugar.

- The first recipe for macaroni and cheese was published in 1769.

- Corn is used in over 4,000 products, including toothpaste and batteries.

- The world's hottest chili pepper, the Carolina Reaper, has a Scoville rating of over 2.2 million units.

- Traditional sushi originally fermented for months before being eaten.

- The world's oldest champagne dates back to 1700s France.

- Chia seeds were once a staple of the Aztec diet due to their high nutritional value.

- Soy sauce was first brewed in China over 2,500 years ago.

- Black garlic is aged for weeks to produce a sweet, molasses-like flavor.

- Peanut butter is consumed by over 90% of U.S. households.

- Poutine, a Canadian dish, is made from fries topped with cheese curds and gravy.

- Milk is one of the most hydrating beverages due to its electrolytes and proteins.

- Ancient Greeks and Romans used olive oil as a hair conditioner.

- The world's largest chocolate bar weighed over 12,000 pounds.

- Traditional balsamic vinegar is aged for at least 12 years in wooden barrels.

- Algae is a key ingredient in many ice creams as a stabilizer.

- British sailors were nicknamed "limeys" because they were given limes to prevent scurvy.

- Bees have to visit about 2 million flowers to make one pound of honey.

- Pizza Margherita is said to have been created in honor of Queen Margherita of Italy.

- Persimmons contain tannins, which give them their characteristic astringency.

- The largest serving of French fries weighed over 8,000 pounds.

Human Psychology

- People tend to believe that their own opinions are the majority opinion, a phenomenon called the false consensus effect.

- Humans are wired to recognize faces in everyday objects, like clouds or toast, a tendency known as pareidolia.

- Laughing causes others to laugh too, even if they don't know the reason, which is called contagious laughter.

- Individuals are more likely to wash their hands after using a public restroom if there's another person present.

- The "halo effect" leads people to assume that physically attractive individuals also have other positive qualities.

- When in a hurry, people often choose the shortest checkout line, but end up waiting longer due to processing times.

- The "IKEA effect" means people value items they've assembled themselves higher than pre-made ones.

- Humans are more likely to remember negative experiences than positive ones due to the negativity bias.

- People often overestimate how much others are noticing them, a psychological phenomenon called the spotlight effect.

- When in a group, individuals tend to take fewer risks because of shared responsibility, known as the diffusion of responsibility.

- People often mimic each other's postures and gestures during conversation without realizing it.

- When reading texts in all caps, people interpret it as shouting or aggressive behavior.

- In loud environments, humans often lean in and shout directly into the other person's ear, which doesn't help with understanding.

- The "Bystander Effect" means individuals are less likely to help someone in need if others are present.

- People can "see" movement in static images if they stare at them long enough, called the Troxler effect.

- People yawn more frequently when others around them yawn, a phenomenon known as contagious yawning.

- When trying to retrieve a memory, people sometimes "blank out" if put under pressure, a phenomenon known as the "tip of the tongue" state.

- People tend to exaggerate their achievements and downplay their failures, known as the self-serving bias.

- Humans often remember details about others better than themselves due to the observer effect.

- When people hear a song that they like, they sometimes experience chills or goosebumps, known as frisson.

- People will often continue eating stale snacks if they're placed in front of them, out of habit or availability bias.

- When buying items, people frequently focus on the cost savings rather than the absolute price.

- Individuals often listen to sad music when feeling down, even though it seems counterintuitive.

- The majority of people think they are better drivers than average, a cognitive bias called illusory superiority.

- People will often conform to group opinions, even if they believe differently, to avoid social rejection (Asch conformity experiment).

- When stressed, people tend to fidget, touch their face, or play with their hair as a self-soothing mechanism.

- People often yawn when they see others yawning, due to a phenomenon called contagious yawning.

- When presented with too many choices, people often choose nothing at all due to analysis paralysis.

- When recounting events, people tend to overestimate their role and importance, known as egocentric bias.

- Individuals often prefer familiar things and people due to the mere exposure effect.

- People are more likely to remember the first and last items in a list than those in the middle, a tendency called the serial position effect.

- People frequently mistake confidence for competence, even when it's unwarranted.

- When someone says "don't think about it," people are more likely to think about it due to the white bear effect.

- The "placebo effect" means that people can feel real health benefits even from inactive substances, as long as they believe in the treatment.

- People are more inclined to agree with statements about themselves that are flattering, even if they're vague or generalized, called the Barnum effect.

- Humans sometimes experience "phantom vibrations," thinking their phone is vibrating even when it's not.

- People are more likely to believe misinformation if it's presented as coming from an authority figure or repeated often.

- People find it easier to lie if they're communicating through text rather than speaking face-to-face.

- When people receive a compliment, they tend to offer one in return due to reciprocity norms.

- People are more inclined to share bad news than good, often out of a need to vent or seek validation.

- When people are hungry, they tend to overestimate how much food they can eat.

- Individuals often believe they can remember past events accurately, but memories can change over time.

- When given a difficult task, people often put it off for easier tasks, a behavior known as procrastination.

- People are often influenced by how information is framed, whether positively or negatively.

- The "endowment effect" leads people to value things they own higher than things they don't.

- People are often less likely to listen attentively when they are preparing a rebuttal or counterargument.

- Humans are prone to see patterns in random data, a phenomenon called apophenia.

- People tend to trust individuals who smile and make eye contact more than those who don't.

- Individuals are more likely to remember significant emotional events than mundane daily activities.

- When witnessing a crime, people often create false memories by filling in details that weren't observed firsthand.

- People sometimes lie to avoid social awkwardness, even when honesty is expected or valued.

Dinosaurs are Awesome

- The largest dinosaur, Argentinosaurus, could weigh up to 100 tons, as much as 14 African elephants.

- Some dinosaurs, like Velociraptor, were feathered, providing insulation and possibly used for display or flight.

- The smallest known dinosaur, Microraptor, was about the size of a crow and could glide between trees.

- The name "dinosaur" means "terrible lizard," coined by Sir Richard Owen in 1842.

- The fossilized remains of dinosaur eggs have revealed that some species nested in colonies.

- Tyrannosaurus rex had a bite force of over 12,000 pounds per square inch, more powerful than any modern land animal.

- Some paleontologists believe that Stegosaurus had a second brain-like structure in its hip region.

- Ankylosaurus had a club-like tail that it could use to defend itself against predators.

- Most dinosaur species were herbivores, with only a minority being carnivores.

- Sauropods like Brachiosaurus could live up to 100 years due to their massive size.

- Scientists have discovered that some dinosaurs could digest food with the help of stones, known as gastroliths, in their stomachs.

- The horned dinosaur Triceratops had three facial horns and a bony frill, possibly for mating displays or defense.

- Carnotaurus, a meat-eating dinosaur, had tiny arms and a pair of distinctive bull-like horns on its head.

- Fossil evidence shows that some dinosaurs suffered from diseases like arthritis and bone infections.

- The fossilized nests of some dinosaurs contain eggs arranged in a circular pattern, suggesting organized nesting behavior.

- Hadrosaurids, or duck-billed dinosaurs, had hundreds of teeth that were continuously replaced throughout their lives.

- The spikes on the tail of Stegosaurus are known as the "thagomizer," after a joke in a Gary Larson comic strip.

- Fossils of dinosaur skin impressions suggest that some species had scales, much like modern reptiles.

- Spinosaurus had a distinctive sail on its back, possibly used for thermoregulation or display.

- Paleontologists often identify new dinosaur species based on differences in skull structure and teeth.

- Some scientists believe that birds evolved directly from small, feathered theropod dinosaurs.

- The first complete dinosaur skeleton discovered was that of Iguanodon in the early 19th century.

- The fearsome predator Giganotosaurus was longer than T. rex but likely not as heavily built.

- The longest dinosaur, Diplodocus, could reach lengths of over 90 feet, with its long neck and tail.

- Ceratosaurus had a distinctive horn on its nose, which might have been used for display or combat.

- Oviraptor was initially thought to be an egg thief but is now believed to have been brooding its own eggs.

- The fossilized footprints of some theropods suggest that they could run at speeds over 25 mph.

- The duck-billed Edmontosaurus could live in herds, as evidenced by bone beds containing hundreds of individuals.

- Dinosaurs laid eggs, and some species are believed to have brooded their nests like modern birds.

- The tallest dinosaur ever discovered was Sauroposeidon, which could reach over 60 feet in height with its neck.

- Scientists have identified over 1,000 different species of dinosaurs to date, with more being discovered regularly.

- Theropod dinosaurs like Allosaurus had serrated teeth adapted to slicing through flesh.

- The thick-skulled Pachycephalosaurus may have used its domed head for head-butting competitions.

- Ankylosaurids had armored plates covering their backs, providing protection against predators.

- Some species of raptors were about the size of modern birds and may have hunted in packs.

- The climate during the Mesozoic Era was much warmer and more humid than today, with lush forests and high sea levels.

- Maiasaura is known as the "good mother lizard" because it showed evidence of caring for its young in nests.

- The extinction event that wiped out the dinosaurs also affected marine reptiles and flying pterosaurs.

- Hadrosaurs had distinctive crests that likely played a role in vocalization and communication.

- Some herbivorous dinosaurs, like Euoplocephalus, had protective bony eyelids.

- The fossilized "mummies" of some dinosaurs have preserved their skin, scales, and even muscles.

- The asteroid impact that led to the extinction of non-avian dinosaurs 66 million years ago created the Chicxulub Crater, which is over 90 miles wide.

- Dinosaurs ruled the Earth for over 160 million years, from the Triassic to the end of the Cretaceous period.

- Dinosaurs roamed all seven continents, including Antarctica, which was much warmer during their time.

- Scientists have discovered that some dinosaurs changed color as they aged or with the seasons, much like modern reptiles.

Earth and its Continents

- Earth's magnetic north pole is slowly drifting towards Russia at a rate of about 25 miles per year.

- The deepest point on Earth, the Mariana Trench, is deeper than Mount Everest is tall.

- Earth once had a second moon that eventually collided with the existing Moon, creating its rugged far side.

- The continents move at the same rate as fingernail growth due to tectonic activity.

- Canada has the most lakes of any country, with about 60% of the world's natural lakes.

- Earth's solid inner core is as hot as the surface of the Sun, reaching temperatures over 5,000°C.

- There are approximately 3 trillion trees on Earth, almost half as many as there were before human civilization.

- Lightning strikes the Earth about 100 times per second, resulting in over 8 million strikes daily.

- Earth's rotation is gradually slowing, meaning days are getting longer by about 1.7 milliseconds per century.

- There are places where tectonic plates are separating, like Iceland's Silfra fissure, allowing divers to swim between continents.

- Lake Hillier in Australia is bright pink due to the presence of salt-loving algae and bacteria.

- About 70% of Earth's freshwater is locked up in glaciers and ice caps.

- The Earth's crust is broken into pieces called tectonic plates, which float on the molten mantle layer.

- The Dead Sea is shrinking rapidly, by about three feet per year, due to human activities and natural causes.

- Africa is the only continent that stretches from the northern temperate to southern temperate zones.

- Australia is the driest inhabited continent, with over 70% of its land classified as arid or semi-arid.

- Asia is the largest continent and hosts the tallest mountain (Mount Everest) and the lowest point on land (Dead Sea).

- Europe has the highest population density among the continents and the most diverse linguistic landscape.

- Antarctica, the coldest continent, is covered by ice sheets that hold nearly 60% of the world's freshwater.

- North America has the longest coastline of any continent due to its complex geography with islands and peninsulas.

- South America has the world's largest river by discharge (Amazon River) and the driest desert (Atacama Desert).

- Greenland, the world's largest island, is geographically part of North America but politically part of Europe.

- Madagascar is the world's fourth-largest island and hosts a unique range of wildlife found nowhere else.

- The Sahara Desert is the largest hot desert on Earth and spans across 10 countries in Africa.

- The Andes is the world's longest mountain range, stretching over 4,300 miles along South America's western coast.

- Australia is home to the Great Barrier Reef, the largest coral reef system and one of the world's natural wonders.

- Europe is the only continent without a desert, but it has diverse climates from polar to Mediterranean.

- The Amazon rainforest is the largest tropical rainforest, covering nearly 40% of South America.

- Antarctica is technically a desert because of its extremely low annual precipitation, despite being covered in ice.

- The Ural Mountains form a natural boundary between Europe and Asia, extending through Russia.

- Lake Baikal in Siberia is the deepest and oldest freshwater lake, holding about 20% of the world's unfrozen freshwater.

- Mount Kilimanjaro in Tanzania is Africa's highest peak and the world's tallest free-standing mountain.

- The Great Lakes of North America contain over 20% of the world's surface freshwater.

- The largest sand desert, the Rub' al Khali, also known as the "Empty Quarter," is located on the Arabian Peninsula.

- Europe's smallest country is Vatican City, which is also the world's smallest independent state.

- The Himalayas are the youngest mountain range on Earth, still growing as the Indian Plate collides with the Eurasian Plate.

- The Danube River flows through ten European countries, more than any other river in the world.

- The world's longest river system, the Nile, flows through 11 countries before reaching the Mediterranean Sea.

- The Dead Sea, located between Jordan and Israel, is Earth's lowest point on land at over 1,400 feet below sea level.

- The Ring of Fire, a horseshoe-shaped area of seismic activity in the Pacific Ocean, has over 450 volcanoes.

- Asia is home to the world's most populous countries, China and India, each with over a billion people.

- Australia has more than 10,000 beaches, offering diverse coastal landscapes and marine life.

- The Alps, the largest mountain range in Europe, are home to some of the world's premier ski resorts.

- Africa's Lake Victoria is the largest tropical lake in the world and the second-largest freshwater lake by surface area.

- The Mariana Trench, in the western Pacific Ocean, is the world's deepest point, reaching over 36,000 feet.

- The Sahara Desert expands and contracts due to climatic fluctuations, affecting livelihoods across North Africa.

- Europe has the greatest number of international borders due to the continent's small size and numerous countries.

- The Amazon Basin is home to over 400 billion trees and supports one of the highest biodiversity levels on Earth.

- The longest railway line, the Trans-Siberian Railway, runs across Russia from Moscow to Vladivostok.

- Madagascar has more than 90% of its wildlife species found nowhere else, including lemurs and baobab trees.

- Greenland is mostly covered by ice sheets, with only a small portion of its land suitable for habitation.

- The Mississippi River, the longest river in North America, drains water from 32 U.S. states and two Canadian provinces.

- Africa's Victoria Falls, one of the largest and most famous waterfalls, is known as "The Smoke That Thunders."

- South America is home to the world's largest salt flats, Salar de Uyuni, located in Bolivia.

- Europe's Rhine River flows through six countries and has been a major trade route for centuries.

- The Arctic Ocean, Earth's smallest and shallowest ocean, is largely covered by ice for most of the year.

- The Great Victoria Desert is Australia's largest desert, located in the country's remote central region.

- The Appalachian Mountains, one of North America's oldest mountain ranges, stretch from Canada to Alabama.

- Africa's Serengeti ecosystem is famous for the annual migration of over 1 million wildebeest.

- The Mediterranean Sea is the world's largest inland sea, bordered by three continents.

- The Gulf of Mexico, the world's largest gulf, borders the southeastern United States and eastern Mexico.

- Iceland, located on the Mid-Atlantic Ridge, is known for its geothermal activity and numerous hot springs.

- The Great Rift Valley, a tectonic fault stretching from the Middle East to Mozambique, is a site of volcanic activity.

- The Atacama Desert in Chile is the driest non-polar desert, with some weather stations never recording rainfall.

- The Nile Delta supports fertile agricultural land in an otherwise arid region, contributing to Egypt's history.

- The Himalayas include over 100 peaks that exceed 7,200 meters (23,600 feet), including Mount Everest.

- Lake Titicaca, on the border of Bolivia and Peru, is the highest navigable lake in the world.

- The European Union includes 27 countries that share a common currency and have eliminated internal border controls.

- Antarctica's Larsen Ice Shelf collapsed in 2002 due to rising temperatures, an event linked to climate change.

- The Tigris and Euphrates rivers in the Middle East were central to the development of ancient Mesopotamian civilization.

- The Daintree Rainforest in Australia is one of the oldest tropical rainforests, dating back over 100 million years.

- Hawaii's Mauna Kea is the tallest mountain if measured from its underwater base to its summit, surpassing Mount Everest.

- The North Sea, bordered by several European countries, is home to significant oil and natural gas reserves.

- The vast tundra region in Russia, Canada, and Scandinavia remains frozen for most of the year.

- The Southern Ocean is Earth's newest recognized ocean, defined in 2000 to encompass the waters around Antarctica.

- Mount McKinley, also known as Denali, is North America's highest peak at over 20,300 feet.

- The Caucasus Mountains between Europe and Asia are home to Mount Elbrus, the highest peak in Europe.

- The Caribbean Sea, with its coral reefs and clear waters, attracts millions of tourists annually.

- The Pampas in Argentina and Uruguay are fertile lowlands ideal for cattle ranching and grain farming.

- The Volga River is Europe's longest river and a major transport route for Russia.

- The Mediterranean climate, found in parts of Europe, Africa, and California, is characterized by hot, dry summers and mild, wet winters.

- The Himalayas are still rising by a few millimeters each year as the Indian and Eurasian plates collide.

- The Namib Desert, one of the world's oldest deserts, is home to towering sand dunes that stretch for miles.

- The Mississippi-Missouri River system is the fourth-longest river system globally, vital to U.S. commerce.

- New Zealand is known for its fjords, geysers, and diverse landscapes, including the Southern Alps.

- The Alps contain many glaciers that provide freshwater to millions of Europeans.

- Australia's Murray-Darling Basin is a major agricultural region and the continent's longest river system.

- Russia is the world's largest country by land area, spanning 11 time zones and two continents.

- Norway's Svalbard archipelago is a key Arctic research base and home to the Global Seed Vault.

- The Ganges River is considered sacred by millions of Hindus and plays a central role in Indian culture.

- The Okavango Delta in Botswana is a vast inland delta that supports a unique ecosystem.

- The Baltic Sea, bordered by nine European nations, is connected to the North Sea via canals.

- The Rocky Mountains, running through the western U.S. and Canada, are known for their scenic national parks.

- The Kalahari Desert is not a true desert but a semi-arid region home to diverse wildlife.

- Greenland's ice sheet is the second-largest in the world and is rapidly melting due to climate change.

Interesting History Facts

- The shortest war in history was between Britain and Zanzibar on August 27, 1896. Zanzibar surrendered after 38 minutes.

- The Great Fire of London in 1666 killed only six people but destroyed over 13,000 homes.

- Cleopatra VII of Egypt lived closer in time to the first moon landing than to the construction of the Great Pyramid of Giza.

- The Eiffel Tower was initially criticized for its design but has become one of the world's most recognizable landmarks.

- The Library of Alexandria, one of the greatest libraries of the ancient world, was destroyed in a series of fires over centuries.

- The world's first university, Al-Qarawiyyin, was founded in 859 AD in Fez, Morocco, by a woman named Fatima al-Fihri.

- The first recorded Olympics were held in 776 BC in ancient Greece and included only one event: a footrace.

- The world's oldest known writing system, cuneiform, originated in Mesopotamia over 5,000 years ago.

- The Taj Mahal was built by Mughal Emperor Shah Jahan in memory of his wife Mumtaz Mahal and took over 20 years to complete.

- The first known coins were minted in Lydia (modern-day Turkey) around 600 BC.

- The Battle of Hastings in 1066 marked the beginning of Norman rule in England, leading to significant cultural changes.

- Ancient Rome had a sewer system called the Cloaca Maxima, which is still partly operational today.

- The Magna Carta, signed in 1215, is considered one of the first documents to outline individual rights.

- Genghis Khan founded the Mongol Empire, which became the largest contiguous land empire in history.

- The Great Wall of China was built over centuries to protect against invasions from northern tribes.

- The Roman Colosseum could hold up to 50,000 spectators and hosted gladiator battles and mock sea battles.

- The Rosetta Stone, discovered in 1799, was key to deciphering Egyptian hieroglyphs.

- Christopher Columbus's expeditions led to lasting contact between the Old World and the New World, beginning the Columbian Exchange.

- Johannes Gutenberg's invention of the movable-type printing press revolutionized the spread of information.

- The Black Death, a bubonic plague pandemic in the 14th century, killed an estimated 25-30 million people in Europe.

- The first successful flight of the Wright brothers in 1903 lasted only 12 seconds and covered 120 feet.

- The Berlin Wall, which divided East and West Berlin, fell in 1989 after nearly three decades of separating families.

- The 1918 Spanish flu pandemic infected one-third of the world's population and killed an estimated 50 million people.

- The Byzantine Empire, the eastern half of the Roman Empire, lasted for over 1,100 years.

- The first artificial satellite, Sputnik 1, was launched by the Soviet Union in 1957, marking the start of the space age.

- Leonardo da Vinci's "The Last Supper" took four years to complete and began to deteriorate within 20 years.

- The Hundred Years' War between England and France lasted 116 years, from 1337 to 1453.

- The Emancipation Proclamation, issued by Abraham Lincoln in 1863, declared all slaves in Confederate territory free.

- The Irish Potato Famine in the 1840s caused mass starvation and led to widespread emigration to the United States.

- The Titanic sank in 1912 on its maiden voyage after hitting an iceberg, resulting in the deaths of over 1,500 people.

- The Code of Hammurabi, dating to around 1754 BC, is one of the earliest known sets of laws.

- The original Olympic Games were held in honor of Zeus, the king of the Greek gods.

- The oldest known musical instrument, a flute made from a bird bone, is over 35,000 years old.

- The Cuban Missile Crisis in 1962 brought the United States and the Soviet Union to the brink of nuclear war.

- The construction of the Panama Canal, completed in 1914, transformed global trade by connecting the Atlantic and Pacific Oceans.

- The medieval English practice of "trial by ordeal" determined guilt by subjecting the accused to dangerous tests.

- Marco Polo's travels to Asia in the 13th century opened new trade routes and inspired European exploration.

- Napoleon Bonaparte crowned himself Emperor of the French in 1804 and conquered much of Europe before his defeat at Waterloo.

- The ancient city of Pompeii was buried under volcanic ash after Mount Vesuvius erupted in AD 79, preserving it for centuries.

- The Mayan civilization developed a complex calendar system that predicted solar eclipses and other astronomical events.

- The Great Depression of the 1930s was a global economic crisis that affected millions of lives.

- The Suez Canal, opened in 1869, provided a direct route for ships between Europe and Asia.

- The Great Zimbabwe was a medieval African city known for its impressive stone architecture.

- The Indus Valley Civilization, which flourished around 2500 BC, had advanced urban planning and sewage systems.

- Mahatma Gandhi led the nonviolent movement for Indian independence from British rule in the mid-20th century.

- The Battle of Stalingrad in World War II was one of the bloodiest battles in history, with over 2 million casualties.

- The Renaissance, beginning in Italy in the 14th century, was a cultural revival of art, science, and literature.

- The Qin Dynasty, which unified China in 221 BC, is known for building the Terracotta Army to protect the emperor's tomb.

- The Viking Leif Erikson reached North America nearly 500 years before Columbus.

- The Roman Empire's Pax Romana was a period of relative peace and stability lasting about 200 years.

- The Great Famine of 1315-1317 devastated Europe, killing millions and leading to widespread social unrest.

- In ancient Egypt, servants were sometimes buried with pharaohs to accompany them in the afterlife.

- Roman Emperor Caligula tried to make his horse, Incitatus, a consul, one of the highest political offices.

- In medieval times, people believed the "four humors" controlled health and personality: blood, phlegm, yellow bile, and black bile.

- Peter the Great of Russia imposed a tax on beards to encourage Western-style grooming practices.

- In the 17th century, tulip bulbs became so valuable in the Netherlands that they were used as currency, leading to a market crash known as "tulip mania."

- During the Great Emu War in Australia in 1932, soldiers used machine guns to try to control the emu population but ultimately failed.

- The Great Emu War was not the only strange battle: The Pig War of 1859 nearly led to conflict between the U.S. and Britain over a pig shot by an American farmer.

- King Charles VI of France believed he was made of glass and was terrified he would shatter.

- President Andrew Jackson once had a 1,400-pound block of cheese placed in the White House for visitors to snack on.

- Catherine the Great of Russia tried to establish a colony in California in the 18th century.

- The British navy created a special unit called the "Pigeon Corps" to carry messages during World War I.

- Before the Gregorian calendar was adopted in 1582, people in many European countries believed New Year's Day was in March.

- At the height of Prohibition in the United States, the government poisoned industrial alcohol to discourage illegal drinking, causing thousands of deaths.

- The Aztec civilization believed that human sacrifices were necessary to keep the sun moving and maintain cosmic order.

- In ancient Rome, wealthy citizens would often have vomitoriums next to their dining rooms to vomit and continue eating.

- In the 19th century, many people believed mummies could cure ailments, leading to a practice known as "mummy unwrapping parties."

- Napoleon Bonaparte wrote a romance novel called "Clisson et Eugénie" before becoming Emperor of France.

- During World War II, the Allies used inflatable tanks and fake radio signals to deceive the Germans about the location of the D-Day invasion.

- The French Revolutionary Calendar, used during the French Revolution, had 10-day weeks to reduce the frequency of religious observance.

- Egyptian pharaoh Pepi II disliked flies so much that he kept slaves covered in honey nearby to attract them away from him.

- In the 1920s, the U.S. had a massive helium reserve, leading to a brief fad for helium-filled, high-pitched voices.

- The ancient Romans had a form of toothpaste made from crushed bones and oyster shells.

- The word "vandalism" originates from the Vandals, an ancient tribe that sacked Rome in AD 455.

- Some English medieval kings kept elephants and other exotic animals in the Tower of London as status symbols.

- Ancient Greek physicians believed hysteria was caused by a "wandering uterus" and treated it with strong-smelling substances.

- During the Qing Dynasty in China, high-ranking officials were required to wear long fingernails to show they did no manual labor.

- The Earl of Oxford, Edward de Vere, was once so embarrassed after breaking wind in front of Queen Elizabeth I that he left England for seven years.

- In 1811, a series of earthquakes along the New Madrid fault line reversed the flow of the Mississippi River.

- In ancient China, royalty would sometimes be buried with miniature terracotta armies to protect them in the afterlife.

- Russian mystic Grigori Rasputin survived several assassination attempts before finally being drowned in a river in 1916.

- In the early 20th century, people believed that radium had health benefits, leading to radioactive toothpaste, makeup, and drinking water.

- Some medieval castles had "murder holes" above their gates, used to pour boiling oil or stones on attackers.

- Aztec priests often used obsidian blades so sharp that they could cut through a human heart in one stroke.

- During World War II, the Japanese Imperial Army built an elaborate system of underground tunnels on Iwo Jima.

- Renaissance painter Michelangelo secretly painted insults about the Pope into his frescoes in the Sistine Chapel.

- The ancient Greeks used powdered mouse brains as toothpaste, believing it would whiten their teeth.

- The ancient Romans were so obsessed with public baths that some emperors built them in the middle of the city.

- In the late 19th century, the "phantom limb" phenomenon was believed to be a form of spirit possession.

- The War of Jenkins' Ear, a conflict between Britain and Spain, began after a British captain had his ear cut off by Spanish coastguards.

- The Inca Empire used a system of knotted strings called quipu to record data and keep track of census information.

- The ancient Egyptians sometimes used crocodile dung as a contraceptive.

- Viking warriors would often file their teeth into points to intimidate their enemies.

- The first known contraceptive was made from crocodile dung and fermented dough in ancient Egypt.

Sports and Games

- The longest tennis match in history lasted over 11 hours across three days, played between John Isner and Nicolas Mahut at Wimbledon in 2010.

- Cricket matches can last up to five days in the Test format and still end in a draw, unlike most other sports.

- The Olympic Games have ancient roots dating back to 776 BC, originally featuring only a single footrace.

- In chess, there are more possible game variations than the number of atoms in the observable universe.

- Polo is one of the world's oldest team sports, believed to have originated in Persia over 2,500 years ago.

- The sport of "octopush" is an underwater hockey game where players push a puck across the pool floor.

- In medieval Europe, "real tennis" was played indoors and is considered the precursor to modern lawn tennis.

- Basketball was invented by James Naismith in 1891 as a less injury-prone alternative to football.

- The Aztecs played a game called "tlachtli," which involved getting a rubber ball through a stone hoop without using hands.

- The longest recorded baseball game lasted 33 innings over eight hours, played between the Pawtucket Red Sox and the Rochester Red Wings.

- Sepak takraw, a Southeast Asian sport, resembles volleyball but uses a rattan ball and prohibits hand contact.

- Jai alai, a fast-paced ball game, was originally played by the Basque people and involves throwing a ball at over 150 mph.

- Croquet was banned in Boston in the 19th century because it was deemed a "waste of time."

- The ancient Greeks and Romans played a game called "episkyros," which is considered a precursor to modern soccer.

- The shortest boxing match in history lasted only four seconds when a boxer was disqualified for a low blow.

- In early forms of rugby, teams could have up to 100 players, leading to chaotic and often violent matches.

- Competitive eating is recognized as a sport, with champions consuming hot dogs, pies, and more in record times.

- Tug of war was once an Olympic event but was discontinued after the 1920 Antwerp Games.

- The first Super Bowl commercial cost $42,000 for a 30-second spot; today's commercials cost over $5 million for the same duration.

- The longest Monopoly game on record lasted for 70 straight days.

- The Olympic marathon distance of 26.2 miles was standardized based on the 1908 London Games to accommodate a route from Windsor Castle to the Olympic Stadium.

- Bocce is an ancient Italian game similar to bowling, with evidence of it being played as early as 5200 BC.

- Korfball, a Dutch invention, is a mixed-gender sport that resembles basketball and netball.

- The FIFA World Cup is the most-watched sporting event globally, attracting billions of viewers.

- Table tennis or ping-pong was once banned in the Soviet Union because it was considered a health hazard.

- The first recorded competitive swimming races were held in Japan in 36 BC.

- The first game of basketball was played with a soccer ball and peach baskets as goals.

- In sumo wrestling, athletes throw salt into the ring before a match to purify it according to Shinto beliefs.

- The Ryder Cup, a golf tournament between the U.S. and Europe, was started in 1927 and remains one of the few non-monetary competitions.

- The game of "rock-paper-scissors" originated in China over 2,000 years ago.

- Kabaddi, an Indian team sport, requires players to tag opponents while holding their breath and chanting "kabaddi."

- The longest golf course in the world, measuring 1,365 miles, is located across the Nullarbor Plain in Australia.

- "Haxey Hood," a medieval game played in England, involves pushing a large leather tube through the streets.

- The Indianapolis 500, an American car race, was first held in 1911 and remains the largest single-day sporting event.

- Horse racing dates back to ancient Babylon and is often called the "sport of kings."

- The 1900 Paris Olympics included live pigeon shooting as an event, which was later discontinued.

- The ancient Mesoamerican ball game of "pok-ta-pok" required players to use their hips to keep a rubber ball in play.

- Baseball's "seventh-inning stretch" tradition was popularized after U.S. President William Howard Taft stood up during a game in 1910.

- The world's longest-running marathon race, the Boston Marathon, was first run in 1897.

- The International Olympic Committee initially refused to include the high jump and javelin throw due to safety concerns.

- The original rules of golf were codified in 1744 by the Honourable Company of Edinburgh Golfers.

- The longest game of cricket, called a "timeless Test," could last for several days until a result was achieved.

- "Bossaball" is a sport that combines volleyball, soccer, and gymnastics, played on an inflatable court with trampolines.

- In chess, a game played between two grandmasters can be considered a "draw" if neither player can force a win.

- The first Olympic Games with a women's event were the 1900 Paris Olympics, featuring tennis and golf.

- Rugby was allegedly invented when a student picked up the ball and ran with it during a soccer match.

- The world record for the most consecutive push-ups is 10,507, set by Minoru Yoshida in 1980.

- "Buzkashi," a Central Asian sport, involves players on horseback trying to carry a goat carcass to a scoring area.

- The Harlem Globetrotters, known for their basketball tricks, have played in over 120 countries since their formation in 1926.

- In soccer, players can receive a red card and be sent off for biting an opponent or throwing an object onto the field.

Mysteries, Myths and Legends

- The Loch Ness Monster is a mythical creature said to inhabit Scotland's Loch Ness, with sightings reported for centuries but no scientific proof of its existence.

- The Mothman, a creature with red eyes and wings, was reportedly seen in Point Pleasant, West Virginia, before the Silver Bridge collapse in 1967.

- The Minotaur, a half-man, half-bull monster, was believed to be imprisoned in a labyrinth on Crete, demanding human sacrifices.

- The legend of El Dorado describes a golden city that inspired countless expeditions, but no trace of it has ever been found.

- In the Arthurian legends, Excalibur is a magical sword that King Arthur pulled from a stone or received from the Lady of the Lake.

- In Japanese folklore, kitsune are foxes that can shapeshift into humans and possess powerful magical abilities.

- The story of Atlantis, described by Plato, suggests a highly advanced civilization that was submerged after a catastrophic event.

- The Phoenix, a mythical bird, is believed to burst into flames upon death and be reborn from its ashes.

- The Bermuda Triangle is believed to be the site of unexplained disappearances of ships and aircraft, leading to various supernatural theories.

- The Dyatlov Pass incident saw nine hikers perish mysteriously in the Russian wilderness, with theories ranging from avalanches to UFOs.

- The Kraken is a legendary sea monster believed to dwell off the coast of Norway and drag ships to their doom.

- The Lost Dutchman's Gold Mine is a supposed treasure trove hidden in Arizona's Superstition Mountains.

- The Chupacabra is a creature of Latin American folklore said to drink the blood of livestock and leave distinctive puncture marks.

- The Banshee, in Irish mythology, is a spirit whose wailing heralds the death of a family member.

- The legend of Robin Hood involves a heroic outlaw who stole from the rich to give to the poor in medieval England.

- The Green Children of Woolpit appeared in medieval England, speaking a strange language and claiming to come from an underground world.

- The Codex Gigas, or "Devil's Bible," is a medieval manuscript believed to have been created with the help of the devil.

- In Norse mythology, Jörmungandr is a giant serpent that encircles the world and will be involved in the end-of-times battle, Ragnarök.

- The story of the Yeti, also called the "Abominable Snowman," describes a large, ape-like creature dwelling in the Himalayas.

- The Nazca Lines are mysterious geoglyphs in Peru depicting animals and shapes, visible only from the air.

- The Bell Witch haunting is an American legend of a vengeful spirit tormenting the Bell family in Tennessee during the 19th century.

- The Thunderbird, a Native American legend, is a supernatural bird capable of summoning storms.

- The lost Roanoke Colony vanished mysteriously in the late 16th century, leaving only the word "Croatoan" as a clue.

- The legend of La Llorona tells of a weeping woman who haunts rivers, searching for her lost children.

- The Mary Celeste was found adrift in 1872 with its cargo intact but no trace of its crew.

- In Greek mythology, Medusa was a Gorgon with snakes for hair whose gaze could turn people to stone.

- Spring-Heeled Jack, a Victorian urban legend, was said to have the ability to leap great distances and terrorize Londoners.

- The Somerton Man, found dead on an Australian beach in 1948, had a mysterious book with an unsolved code.

- In Chinese folklore, the Jade Rabbit lives on the moon and prepares the elixir of life for the immortals.

- In Mayan mythology, the Hero Twins descended to the underworld to play a ballgame against the lords of death.

- In Finnish folklore, the Sampo was a magical artifact that could bring good fortune to its possessor.

- The Jersey Devil is a legendary creature said to inhabit the Pine Barrens of New Jersey, with sightings dating back to the 18th century.

- The Phaistos Disc, a clay artifact from ancient Crete, contains symbols that remain undeciphered.

- The Wendigo is a malevolent spirit in Native American folklore that possesses people, driving them to cannibalism.

- The Kraken, said to live off the coast of Norway, is described in Nordic folklore as a giant octopus or squid.

- The cursed Hope Diamond, believed to bring misfortune to its owners, was once owned by Marie Antoinette and other European royalty.

- The legend of the Flying Dutchman involves a ghost ship that cannot make port and is doomed to sail the seas forever.

- The Roswell Incident of 1947 in New Mexico is thought by many to involve a UFO crash covered up by the government.

- The Easter Island statues, or Moai, were created by the Rapa Nui people, but how they were moved remains a mystery.

- The disappearance of Malaysia Airlines Flight MH370 in 2014 has sparked many theories and remains unsolved.

Insects and Plant Life

- The titan arum, or corpse flower, blooms once every few years and emits a smell like rotting flesh to attract pollinators.

- The sundew is a carnivorous plant that uses sticky droplets on its leaves to trap and digest insects.

- Some plants, like the Venus flytrap, can count how many times an insect touches their sensory hairs before closing.

- Bamboo can grow up to 35 inches per day, making it the fastest-growing plant in the world.

- The honey bee is the only insect that produces food eaten by humans on a large scale, specifically honey.

- The "walking palm" tree in Central and South America can "walk" up to several meters over years by growing new roots in the direction of sunlight.

- The monarch butterfly migrates up to 3,000 miles annually from North America to Central Mexico, using the Sun and magnetic fields to navigate.

- The Rafflesia arnoldii, the largest flower in the world, can reach over 3 feet in diameter and smells like decaying meat.

- Ants can lift and carry objects up to 50 times their body weight due to their unique muscle structure.

- The "sensitive plant" (Mimosa pudica) rapidly folds its leaves when touched to protect itself from herbivores.

- The larvae of the Atlas moth, one of the world's largest moths, can consume entire leaves in minutes.

- The dragon blood tree in Yemen produces a red sap that was historically used as medicine and dye.

- Termites cultivate underground fungi farms in their nests to help break down tough plant fibers for food.

- Some orchids can mimic the appearance and scent of female insects to trick male pollinators into fertilizing them.

- The locust, a type of grasshopper, can form swarms numbering billions of individuals and devastate crops across continents.

- The Wollemi pine, thought extinct for millions of years, was discovered in 1994 in a remote Australian forest.

- The Madagascan comet orchid has a nectar spur up to 11 inches long, accessible only to a moth with a matching proboscis.

- Some ants form living bridges using their bodies to help their colony cross water or other obstacles.

- Certain species of pitcher plants can lure, drown, and digest small mammals like rats and mice.

- The Amazon rainforest is home to over 80,000 plant species, many of which have yet to be scientifically documented.

- Ginkgo biloba, known as the "living fossil," is the only surviving species of a plant group dating back over 200 million years.

- The bombardier beetle sprays a boiling, noxious liquid to deter predators through a chemical reaction inside its body.

- The stinking corpse lily can take up to 10 months to bloom, releasing its foul odor for just a few days to attract flies.

- Leafcutter ants cultivate fungus on chewed leaves to feed their entire colony.

- The giant water lily has leaves that can support a small child and flowers that change color after pollination.

- Aphids can reproduce asexually, producing genetically identical offspring without needing a mate.

- The dragon tree of the Canary Islands bleeds red sap that was once believed to have magical properties.

- The world's smallest flowering plant, Wolffia, is only about the size of a grain of rice and has no leaves or roots.

- The Asian giant hornet, also known as the "murder hornet," can decimate entire honey bee hives in a matter of hours.

- The bristlecone pine, found in North America, is the world's oldest living tree, with individuals over 4,800 years old.

- In tropical rainforests, fig trees rely on specialized wasps to pollinate their flowers and sustain their growth.

- Some cacti grow underground, with only the spines visible above the surface, to protect themselves from extreme heat.

- The jewel beetle's iridescent exoskeleton reflects light in a way that makes it difficult for predators to spot.

- The Venus flytrap requires multiple stimuli within a short time to activate, ensuring it only closes on live prey.

- The corpse flower's powerful scent attracts carrion beetles and flesh flies for pollination, mistaking it for a dead animal.

- The leaf insect uses elaborate camouflage to blend in with foliage, even rocking like a leaf to mimic movement in the wind.

- Some trees can communicate through underground fungal networks, warning each other of insect attacks or drought.

- Male bees, called drones, cannot sting and exist solely to mate with a queen bee.

- The ancient fern Cyathea medullaris has black trunk scales used in traditional Polynesian tattooing.

- Army ants form rafts using their bodies to survive flooding, keeping the queen and larvae safely in the center.

Unbelievable Survival Stories

- Roy Sullivan, a park ranger in the U.S., holds the record for being struck by lightning the most times and surviving. He was struck seven times between 1942 and 1977 and was known as the "Human Lightning Rod." Despite the injuries he sustained from these lightning strikes, Sullivan remarkably survived each incident.

- Frane Selak, a Croatian music teacher, survived a train derailment, a plane crash, a bus accident, two car explosions, and being hit by a bus, earning him the title "world's luckiest man."

- Aron Ralston amputated his own arm after being trapped under a boulder for over five days in a Utah canyon, then hiked to safety.

- Violet Jessop, known as "Miss Unsinkable," survived the sinking of both the Titanic and its sister ship, Britannic, as well as a collision involving another ship, Olympic.

- Juliane Koepcke survived a plane crash in the Amazon rainforest, trekked through the jungle alone for 11 days, and was finally rescued by loggers.

- Hugh Glass was mauled by a grizzly bear in 1823, crawled 200 miles to safety, and sought revenge on his attackers.

- Joe Simpson fell and broke his leg on Siula Grande in the Andes, was left for dead, but managed to crawl back to base camp.

- Poon Lim survived for 133 days on a raft in the Atlantic Ocean after his ship was torpedoed in World War II.

- Apollo 13's crew used the Lunar Module as a lifeboat to return to Earth after an oxygen tank exploded en route to the moon.

- Mauro Prosperi got lost in the Sahara Desert during the Marathon des Sables and wandered for nine days before finding help.

- Tami Oldham Ashcraft sailed through Hurricane Raymond and was left adrift at sea for 41 days after her yacht capsized.

- Harrison Okene was trapped in an air pocket inside a sunken ship for nearly three days before being rescued by divers.

- Steven Callahan drifted for 76 days in a life raft in the Atlantic Ocean after his boat was struck by a whale.

- Beck Weathers was left for dead during the 1996 Mount Everest disaster but managed to descend from the mountain with severe frostbite.

- Alvar Núñez Cabeza de Vaca survived a shipwreck in the Gulf of Mexico and wandered through the southwestern U.S. for eight years.

- Yossi Ghinsberg was lost for three weeks in the Amazon rainforest after a rafting trip went wrong.

- Nando Parrado and Roberto Canessa hiked for ten days across the Andes to get help after their plane crashed, leading to the rescue of 16 survivors.

- José Salvador Alvarenga drifted in the Pacific Ocean for 438 days after a fishing trip gone wrong.

- Annette Herfkens was the sole survivor of a plane crash in Vietnam, enduring eight days in the jungle with injuries and little water.

- Ernest Shackleton and his crew navigated treacherous seas in a lifeboat to reach South Georgia Island after their ship was crushed by ice.

- Vesna Vulović survived a 33,000-foot fall after her plane exploded, holding the record for the highest fall without a parachute.

- Amanda Eller was lost in a Hawaiian forest for 17 days after going for a hike but was found dehydrated and injured.

- Roy Sullivan, a U.S. park ranger, was struck by lightning seven times and survived each incident.

- Ada Blackjack survived two years alone on Wrangel Island in the Arctic after her expedition's leader left to find help.

- Ricky Megee wandered for 71 days through the Australian Outback after being abandoned by his travel companions.

- Ben Carpenter, a paraplegic man in a wheelchair, was stuck on the front grille of a truck and pushed for miles but remained uninjured.

- Tsutomu Yamaguchi survived the atomic bombings of both Hiroshima and Nagasaki within three days and lived to tell the tale.

- Anne Frank and her family evaded capture for over two years by hiding in a secret annex during the Nazi occupation of the Netherlands.

Imprint

MSDKI

195533 N 109th St, Scottsdale, AZ 85255, USA

ISBN: 9798345964958

First Edition
© 2024 Mark Jones

Made in United States
Troutdale, OR
11/21/2024

25160850R00061